curiousabout
BASKETBALL

BY JOE TISCHL

AMICUS

What are you

curious about?

CHAPTER THREE

3

Playing the Game

PAGE

16

Curious About is published by Amicus
P.O. Box 227
Mankato, MN 56002
www.amicuspublishing.us

Copyright © 2024 Amicus.
International copyright reserved in all countries.
No part of this book may be reproduced in any
form without written permission from the publisher.

Editor: Alissa Thielges
Series Designer: Kathleen Petelinsek
Book Designer: Lori Bye
Photo Researcher: Omay Ayres

Library of Congress Cataloging-in-Publication Data
Names: Tischler, Joe, author.
Title: Curious about basketball / by Joe Tischler.
Description: Mankato, MN: Amicus, [2024] | Series: Curious
about sports | Includes bibliographical references and index.
| Audience: Ages 6–9 | Audience: Grades 2–3 | Summary:
"Conversational questions and answers share what kids
can expect when they join a basketball team including what
gear to pack, some basic rules of play, and how a team
works together to score points"—Provided by publisher.
Identifiers: LCCN 2022043954 (print) | LCCN
2022043955 (ebook) | ISBN 9781645493211
(library binding) | ISBN 9781681528458
(paperback) | ISBN 9781645494096 (ebook)
Subjects: LCSH: Basketball—Juvenile literature.
Classification: LCC GV885.1 .T57 2024 (print) | LCC
GV885.1 (ebook) | DDC 796.323–dc21/eng/20220929
LC record available at https://lccn.loc.gov/2022043954
LC ebook record available at https://lccn.loc.gov/2022043955

Getty/Hill Street Studios 14–15, kali9 11, miljko 6–7,
monkeybusinessimages 20–21, Tony Garcia 9; iStock/
FatCamera 5; Shutterstock/Andrey Arkusha 16,
enterlinedesign 17, er ryan 22, 23 (icons), eurobanks
19, Milos Kontic 13, Monkey Business Images 12, Node
Hingprakhon 8, Pressmaster 4, Rawpixel.com cover, 1

Printed in China

CHAPTER ONE

How old do you have to be to play?

You can start really young! There are smaller basketballs for young players. As soon as you can run and hold a ball, you can learn to **dribble** and shoot. When you enter grade school, you can join a team.

...s use one hand to dribble.

DID YOU KNOW?
James Naismith invented basketball in 1891.

Where can I go to play basketball?

Kids practice dr...
in a school gym...

You can play basketball inside or outside parks usually have a basketball court What if it's raining Head Most gyms have c depends on your a to op.

What type of equipment do I need?

Not much at all! Just good athletic shoes and a basketball. If you are on a team, you'll want basketball shoes. They have more weight than regular shoes. The tall sides give your ankles more support.

A one-on-one game is a good way to improve your skills.

CHAPTER TWO

What teams can I play on?

Teams are based on age. Children start joining teams around age seven. See if your school has any after-school **leagues**. Or you can check with your city's community center.

DID YOU KNOW?
People with physical impairments can play basketball in wheelchairs.

Wheelchair basketball is popular around the world.

What position should I play?

Five players are on the court at a time. There are two guards, two forwards, and one center. Shorter players are usually guards. They shoot well from longer distances. Centers are usually taller. It is easier for them to grab **rebounds**. Forwards are good at both shooting and grabbing rebounds.

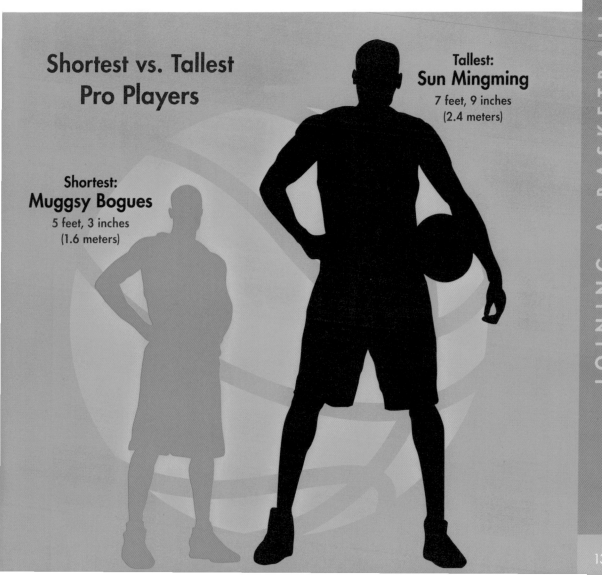

Shortest vs. Tallest Pro Players

Shortest:
Muggsy Bogues
5 feet, 3 inches
(1.6 meters)

Tallest:
Sun Mingming
7 feet, 9 inches
(2.4 meters)

Who will coach my team?

High school coaches are sometimes teachers, too.

Younger players are often coached by parents. It could be your mom or dad! As players get older, coaches are **volunteers**. They usually played basketball and know the game well. In school, trained coaches will lead your team. They put you through practices. They design **plays** during games.

How do I score?

Shoot the ball through the **opponent**'s hoop! Be careful though. The other team's defenders will try to stop you. Dribble around them to take a shot. Or you can pass to a teammate who is open. Baskets are worth two or three points.

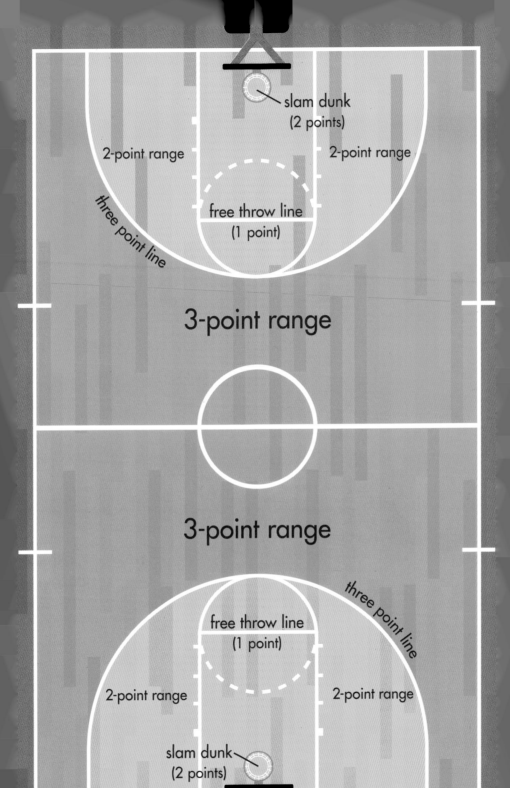

slam dunk
(2 points)

2-point range

2-point range

three point line

free throw line
(1 point)

3-point range

3-point range

free throw line
(1 point)

2-point range

2-point range

three point line

slam dunk
(2 points)

What's a foul?

It's when someone breaks a rule. Usually, a player makes unnecessary contact with an opponent. This could be pushing or grabbing another player. A foul always has a **penalty**. The other team usually gets the ball. Sometimes they also get a **free throw**. You don't want too many fouls in a game. You can get kicked out of the game.

TECHNICAL FOUL

When a player or coach on the court or bench are called for bad behavior or language.

TRAVELING

When a player with the ball takes more than one step without dribbling.

JUMP BALL

When players from both teams have possession of ball at the same time.

PERSONAL FOUL

When a player makes any illegal contact with an opposing player.

CHARGING FOUL

When an offensive player runs into an opponent who is standing still, making no effort to avoid contact.

How long is a game?

It depends on the players' ages. Games are divided into two halves. Each half can be 10 to 20 minutes long. Some leagues divide the halves into quarters, too. Older kids have longer games. In college, there are two 20-minute halves. NBA games have four 12-minute quarters.

High school games have four 8-minute quarters.

ASK MORE QUESTIONS

What basketball drills I can practice at home?

How long do players have until they have to shoot the ball?

Try a BIG QUESTION: How can playing basketball help me stay healthy?

SEARCH FOR ANSWERS

Search the library catalog or the Internet.
A librarian, teacher, or parent can help you.

Using Keywords
Find the looking glass.

Keywords are the most important words in your question.

If you want to know about:
- basketball practice drills, type: BASKETBALL DRILLS
- how long players have to shoot type: BASKETBALL SHOT CLOCK